The Da... ... Of Chronic Overthinking

Strategies For Quieting The Mind And Finding Inner Peace

Dr, Tiffany J. Bozeman

1

CONTENT

4

CHAPTER ONE

Introduction

Overthinking is a widespread issue that millions of individuals experience worldwide. It is a way of thinking when you focus on the same ideas or thoughts for a long time, often to the point of obsession. Although everyone sometimes overthinks, persistent overthinking may be a significant issue that can result in anxiety, sadness, and other mental health problems. This chapter examines the characteristics of overthinking, its root causes, and any possible risks associated with this way of thinking.

The Nature of Overthinking

One sort of cognitive distortion that might result in unfavorable thoughts and emotions is overthinking. It often entails worrying excessively about a certain issue or circumstance, which frequently results in a feeling of tension or anxiety. Overthinkers may find themselves mentally rehearsing the same situations over, seeing the worst-case scenario, and evaluating every potential result.

A certain amount of reflection and analysis may be beneficial, but persistent overthinking can be damaging. It may result in feelings of exhaustion, a lack of concentration, and ineffectiveness. Moreover, overthinking might make it difficult to go to sleep or remain asleep at night.

Causes and Consequences of Chronic Overthinking

Chronic overthinking may have a variety of reasons, such as worry, stress, and previous traumas. Individuals who have gone through tragedy in the past may be more prone to overthinking as a coping mechanism. Similarly to this, anxious individuals may get mired in a loop of overthinking as a means of attempting to foresee prospective issues and prevent unpleasant results.

Many detrimental consequences might arise from persistent overthinking in one's life. Relationship problems, feelings of worry and sadness, and a general decline in quality of life might result from it. Overthinkers may find it challenging to concentrate on their job or enjoy their free time, which may result in frustration and unhappiness.

The Dangers Of Overthinking

Even while it may seem like a harmless habit, overthinking may have detrimental effects on both mental and physical health. Persistent overthinking may have a variety of detrimental impacts, such as:

1. Anxiety: Overthinking may make you feel anxious, which raises your alertness level and puts you at risk for panic attacks.

2. Depression: In addition to increasing overthinking, depression may also develop as a result of unhappiness, hopelessness, and despair.

3. Overthinking may disrupt sleep, making it challenging to go to sleep or remain asleep at night.

4. Persistent overthinking may cause physical health difficulties including migraines, tension headaches, and digestive problems.

5. Decreased Productivity: Thinking too much may get in the way of getting work done and engaging in other activities, which lowers productivity and causes irritation and discontent.

Overthinking is a prevalent issue that may have detrimental effects on both physical and mental health. Persistent overthinking may cause a variety of undesirable side effects, including anxiety, sadness, and sleeplessness. To create successful techniques for dealing with this issue, it is critical to comprehend the nature of overthinking, its origins, and the possible risks associated with this way of thinking. People may escape the destructive cycle of overthinking and live happier, more fulfilled lives by learning to quiet the mind and practice mindfulness.

Overthinking's Effects On Mental Health

Chronic overthinking may significantly affect mental health, which is an important component of total wellness. The relationship between overthinking and anxiety, how it affects mood and behavior, and its bodily consequences are all discussed in this chapter.

Overthinking and Anxiety

One of the most prevalent mental health conditions, anxiety affects millions of individuals worldwide. Overthinking and anxiety are strongly related, and overthinkers may be more susceptible to anxiety symptoms. This is because overthinking may result in elevated arousal and a persistent feeling of concern, which are defining characteristics of anxiety.

Overthinkers may find themselves thinking about every eventuality that may happen, seeing the worst-case scenario, and continually scrutinizing every aspect of their life. This may seem draining and overpowering, causing worry and a sense of helplessness.

How Overthinking Affects Mood and Behavior

The effects of overthinking on emotions and behavior may be profound. Overthinkers may experience irritability, and frustration, and quickly become overwhelmed. Relationship tension and difficulty interacting socially might result from this.

Moreover, overthinking may cause a feeling of helplessness and despair, which might support the development of depression. Overthinkers may find themselves ruminating on unfavorable ideas and feelings, which may create a vicious cycle of unfavorable thinking.

Persistent overthinking's harmful physical effects

Many physical repercussions of persistent overthinking may be seen in the body. The body releases stress chemicals like cortisol and adrenaline when a person is anxious all the time. These hormones may harm the body in several ways, including:

1. Persistent overthinking may cause an elevated heart rate, which can put pressure on the heart and promote the onset of heart disease.

16

2. Digestive Problems: Stress hormones may also affect digestion, causing tummy aches, motion sickness, and other digestive problems.

3. Persistent overthinking may result in muscular tension, which can further exacerbate headaches, neck and shoulder discomfort, and other musculoskeletal issues.

4. Immune system weakened: Stress hormones may impair immunity, leaving a person more prone to disease and infection.

Chronic overthinking may negatively affect both one's physical and mental health. It has a strong connection to anxiety and may have several detrimental emotional and physical impacts. People may lessen the effects of overthinking on their life and enhance their general wellness by being aware of the symptoms and creating appropriate coping mechanisms.

CHAPTER TWO

Techniques For Relaxing The Mind

Some techniques might help calm the mind and foster inner peace. Persistent overthinking can be burdensome and draining. The benefits of mindfulness in reducing overthinking are discussed in this chapter, along with methods for developing awareness via meditation and other activities.

The Value of Mindfulness in Conquering Overthinking

A person who practices mindfulness is present and involved in the time at hand. It helps to bring consciousness to the current moment and lessen the continual stream of thoughts and anxieties, making it a crucial technique for overcoming overthinking.

People may learn to step back from their thoughts and emotions and view them objectively by practicing mindfulness. This may lessen the harmful effects of negative thoughts and emotions on mental health and assist to stop the cycle of overthinking.

Ways to Develop Mindfulness Through Other Practices and Meditation

One of the best methods to develop awareness and calm the mind is meditation. It entails being still while concentrating on your breathing and monitoring your thoughts and feelings without passing judgment.

Yoga, tai chi, and other types of mindful movement are other activities that may aid in developing mindfulness. With the use of these techniques, people may strengthen their connection to their bodies and increase their awareness of bodily sensations, which can serve as an anchor for the present.

How To Remain Focused And Present In The Moment:

Overcoming overthinking requires being mindful of the present and paying attention to the here and now. There are several methods that people may take to be present and concentrated, such as:

1. Deep breathing exercises may help people remain in the present moment by calming their minds and lowering their stress levels.

2. Visualization: People may use visualization methods to create a calm scene in their minds, which can assist to calm the mind and lessen overthinking.

3. Eating mindfully entails paying great attention to the many flavors, textures, and aromas of the food you are consuming. This may assist people in staying in the present and lessen the negative effects of overthinking on eating patterns.

Finding inner calm and eliminating overthinking need the development of mindfulness. People may learn to separate from their thoughts and emotions and be present at the moment by engaging in meditation and other mindfulness practices. This might lessen the negative effects of overthinking on mental health while enhancing general welfare.

Making Good Habits and Routines

Good routines and habits may be effective weapons in the fight against overthinking and the promotion of mental wellness.

This chapter will cover how to create a daily routine that promotes mental health, how to battle overthinking with good habits, and how to remain motivated and dedicated to making positive changes.

The Role Of Healthy Habits In Preventing Overthinking

Good behaviors may ease stress, elevate mood, and advance general well-being. Since they provide structure and regularity, which may help to relax the mind and lessen the influence of unfavorable ideas and emotions, they can also be effective aids in the fight against overthinking.

Regular exercise, a balanced diet, getting adequate sleep, learning relaxation methods, and participating in fun hobbies are all examples of healthy habits. You may build a feeling of stability and balance by implementing these routines into your everyday life, which can help to lessen the negative effects of overthinking on mental health.

How To Create A Mental Health-supportive Daily Routine

It might be difficult to establish a daily routine that improves mental health, but it is crucial for preventing overthinking and enhancing general well-being. Here are some guidelines for establishing a schedule that promotes mental health:

1. Prioritize: Decide what matters most to you and what behaviors and activities will promote your mental health and well-being.

2. Plan your day: Establish a timetable that takes into account your priorities and

leaves time for routine exercise, wholesome food, rest, and fun activities.

3. Be adaptable: Although having a schedule is necessary, it's equally crucial to be adaptable and adjust to changing conditions.

How To Remain Inspired And Committed To Good Change

Motivation and dedication are needed to establish healthy routines and behaviors. Here are some tactics for maintaining your drive and dedication to making a great change:

1. Establish attainable objectives. To make advancement more reasonable, divide your goals into smaller, attainable tasks.

2. Appreciate your victories: To remain inspired and goal-focused, celebrate your accomplishments, no matter how minor.

3. Get support: If you need assistance staying motivated and dedicated to making great changes, ask your family, friends, or a therapist for assistance.

Good routines and habits may be effective weapons in the fight against overthinking and the promotion of mental wellness. People may develop a feeling of stability and balance that can assist to lessen the effects of overthinking on mental health by developing a daily routine that includes regular exercise, good food, relaxation methods, and pleasurable hobbies. People may establish enduring habits and routines that promote their general well-being by being motivated and dedicated to making beneficial changes.

CHAPTER THREE

The Influence Of Self-reflection

Self-reflection is an effective strategy for figuring out our thought processes and growing in self-awareness and insight. This chapter will cover methods for increasing self-awareness and insight, as well as how self-reflection may assist people in letting go of unfavorable thought patterns.

How Self-reflection May Help People Comprehend Their Thought Processes

Self-reflection is a potent technique for gaining insight into our thought processes and the effects they have on our lives. We may start to see patterns and themes that could be causing our negative thought patterns by taking stock of our actions and thoughts. For instance, if we see that we often have negative ideas about ourselves, we may be able to recognize the patterns of perfectionism or self-criticism that are causing these thoughts.

How To Grow Your Self-awareness And Insight

Practice and purpose are necessary for the development of self-awareness and insight. These are some methods for increasing one's awareness of oneself and insight:

1. Putting down our thoughts and emotions in a journal might help us see themes and patterns in our thinking.

2. Mindfulness: Using mindfulness techniques may make us more conscious of our thoughts and emotions as they are occurring right now.

3. Meditation: Meditation may help us become more peaceful and focused, enabling us to think more thoroughly about our actions and ideas.

How to Use Self-Reflection To Break Free From Negative Thinking Habits

Self-reflection is a potent strategy for overcoming destructive thought patterns. We may start to see patterns and themes that could be causing our negative thought patterns by taking stock of our actions and thoughts. We may start formulating plans for escaping these patterns after we have discovered them.

For instance, if we see that we often have negative ideas about ourselves, we may be able to recognize the patterns of perfectionism or self-criticism that are causing these thoughts. When we practice self-compassion or reframe our ideas more positively, we may start to create skills for combating these negative beliefs.

Self-reflection is an effective strategy for figuring out our thought processes and growing in self-awareness and insight. We may start to see patterns and themes that could be causing our negative thought patterns by taking stock of our actions and thoughts. We may start to foster a more upbeat and healthy mentality by devising methods for escaping these destructive routines. Self-reflection has the potential to be a potent technique for fostering mental health and well-being with practice and purpose.

Building A Support System

It may be solitary and lonely to overthink. Yet, by offering a feeling of connection, comprehension, and encouragement, creating a support network may assist people in overcoming overthinking. This chapter will cover how to create a solid support system, how to ask for assistance when you need it, and the significance of social support in overcoming overthinking.

The Significance Of Social Support In Overcoming Overthinking

One important factor in overcoming overthinking is social support. A robust support system may provide a secure and accepting environment where people can express their ideas and emotions, get affirmation and support, and discover fresh approaches to their problems.

According to research, social support may also improve the state of one's mental health. Strong support networks help people deal with stress and adversity and reduce their risk of developing depressive and anxiety symptoms.

Ways For Creating A Powerful Support System

It takes conscious effort and dedication to develop a solid support system. Here are some tips for creating a powerful support system:

1. Determine your needs: Decide what sort of assistance you need first. Do you need someone who can provide you with sound advice and emotional support, or are you seeking someone who can listen and support you emotionally?

2. Contact your friends and family: They may be an excellent source of support. Inform the people you feel comfortable discussing with and who you trust about the kind of help you need.

3. Join a support group: Support groups may provide an opportunity to learn from others who may be facing similar difficulties, as well as a feeling of community and understanding.

4. Get expert assistance: A therapist or counselor may give a private, secure environment for people to explore their ideas and emotions as well as direction and help for overcoming overthinking.

When Assistance Is Required, The Following Steps Should Be Taken

It might be risky and challenging to ask for assistance. Yet it's crucial to keep in mind that asking for help indicates strength, not weakness. Here are some pointers for asking for assistance when you need it:

1. Be upfront and honest when asking for assistance. It's crucial to be open and honest about your difficulties and requirements. This may make it clearer for other people how to assist you.

2. Be clear about the kind of assistance you need, whether it be emotional support, useful counsel, or just a listening ear.

3. Establish limits: It's crucial to specify the kind of help you feel comfortable receiving and to let people know what those boundaries are.

4. Exercise self-compassion: While you seek out assistance, keep in mind to be kind and sympathetic to yourself. Reaching out for assistance may be a challenging and vulnerable experience, but it's a crucial first step on the road to recovery and development.

Creating a support system is essential for overcoming overthinking. Social support may provide an opportunity to learn from others who might be facing comparable difficulties, as well as a feeling of connection, comprehension, and encouragement. People may develop a feeling of resilience and well-being by asking for assistance when they need it and creating a strong support system. They can also learn new strategies for overcoming the difficulties associated with overthinking.

How To Find Inner Peace

The path to inner calm may be difficult, especially for individuals who suffer from persistent overthinking. Nonetheless, it is possible to nurture a feeling of peace and tranquility even amid challenging problems by combining the tactics and approaches covered in earlier chapters. The advantages of inner peace for general health and well-being will be discussed in this chapter along with techniques for achieving and maintaining inner peace and tranquility.

Using all of the techniques for achieving inner quiet:

A mix of physical, mental, and emotional disciplines is necessary to achieve inner peace and tranquility. These are some methods for achieving inner serenity and peace:

1. Mindfulness: Developing awareness via exercises like yoga and meditation may help people remain grounded and in the moment, lowering stress and anxiety.

2. Self-reflection: By reflecting on one's actions and cognitive processes, one

might better comprehend them and find fresh approaches to problems.

3. Developing healthy routines and habits may help people feel more energized and focused. Examples include frequent exercise and a regular sleep schedule.

4. Social support: Establishing a solid support system may foster a feeling of community and understanding as well as provide chances for development and education.

Ways To Be Calm And Quiet Amid Difficulties

Amid difficulties and anxieties, it may be challenging to maintain a calm and serene frame of mind. Here are some pointers for preserving tranquility and inner peace:

1. Take care of yourself by doing things you like and find relaxing, like reading, being in nature, or having a warm bath.

2. Try remaining in the current moment rather than dwelling on the past or the future. This may lessen tension and anxiety.

3. Develop thankfulness: Maintaining a good perspective and lowering stress may be accomplished by focusing on the positive parts of life, such as an appreciation for relationships, health, and individual achievements.

4. Get help: For advice and support during trying times, turn to friends, family, or a mental health professional.

The Advantages Of Inner Peace For General Health And Well-being

Developing inner calm and serenity may have a variety of positive consequences on general health and well-being. The following are a few advantages of inner peace:

1. Decreased stress and anxiety: Having inner peace may help people cope with stress and anxiety better, which lowers the chance of unfavorable health effects.

2. Better sleep: Using relaxation methods and finding inner peace may lead to better sleep, which will give you more energy and concentration throughout the day.

3. More resilience: Those who practice inner peace tend to be more resilient and

have better-coping mechanisms, which makes it simpler for them to deal with difficulties and adversity.

4. More empathy, understanding, and connection in interpersonal interactions may result from inner serenity.

Conclusion

It may be difficult to achieve inner peace and tranquility, but it is possible to do so by combining techniques like mindfulness, self-reflection, constructive routines and habits, and social support. Less stress and anxiety, better sleep, higher resilience, and improved relationships are just a few of the advantages of maintaining a calm and serene state of mind via techniques like self-care, being present, developing appreciation, and getting help. People may lay the groundwork for long-term health, pleasure, and well-being by prioritizing inner calm.